DAY TRADING MADE EASY

How to Day Trade for a Living, become a Profitable Investor and
Build a Passive Income! Includes Swing and Day Trading,
Dividend Investing, Options for Income

SAMUEL DOUGLAS

content within this book has been derived from various sources. Please consult a licensed professional before attempting any techniques outlined in this book.

By reading this document, the reader agrees that under no circumstances is the author responsible for any losses, direct or indirect, which are incurred as a result of the use of information contained within this document, including, but not limited to, errors, omissions, or inaccuracies.

Table of Contents

INTRODUCTION

Thank you so much for purchasing the book. *Why You Should Start Investing in Options, Futures, EFTs, and Forex for a Massive Income.* In this book, we will get you ready for trading.

What this book is all about

Getting started with day trading is a pretty big decision. You can achieve the ideal of bringing in profits with only a few hours a day trading, but that won't be reality for many people that are just beginners and it will be necessary to just stay above the water during the first year and to actually get a feel for what it's like with all the fluctuations. Your only goal during the beginning and the learning stages is to just stay in the game and not to sink. If you still want to undertake this activity, and if you are still interested after this introduction, then day trading just might be for you. It is necessary to have the right knowledge in order to get anywhere.

With this book, you should be able to start day trading right after you have finished reading our Conclusion page, which will make you more than a beginner in the world of stock trading.

What anyone feeling discouraged should know is that anyone can learn how to trade stocks; however, not many people can make a living out of it.

This is because trading is more than just buying when low and selling when high, although this simple rule naturally brings profit if done at the right time and with the right stocks.

But, in order to make the right decision with "selling when high and buying when low," there are many things in between that needs to be learned.

Why you should read this book

We got you covered there as we have compiled a guide with strategies that shouldn't take more than 45 minutes per day for you to complete towards making your first 85.000 dollars in a year with day trading.

Once the knowledge is acquired, the practice can take its turn, leading towards acquiring experience that can, later on, grant you an even higher positive return on a yearly basis – only requiring 45 minutes of your time in a day.

To take you to the point where you can actually join real-time live trading where the real money and real investments are at stake, we first must take you to an inevitable journey through day trading basics – and more!

The "more" means that you will find some simple and basic techniques throughout the chapters of our book that will equip you for the very start of your day trading career that should bring you a significant profit through an almost effortless experience.

In our book, you will learn how to become a skilled day trader, how to interpret charts and follow up on market trends, when to sell and how to buy stocks, which techniques to avoid and which day trading techniques need to be embraced, and much more.

The basics of day trading alongside day trading techniques are also covered in Day Trading for a Living, so you will learn what day trading actually is, who are the participants, and what tools do you need in order to start with and become able to turn your investment into a significant amount of profit.

After you have finished Day Trading for a Living, you should be able to start your day trading sessions immediately, taking off into new experiences of the stock trading market and embracing the opportunity that day trading can bring to those who know where to look for a valuable source of profit.

The most important thing, you will be ready for day trading starting from day one!

CHAPTER 1: WHAT TO KEEP IN MIND WHILE TRADING-DAY 2- BASICS OF SWING TRADING

Swing trading is very common to several investors across the globe. It can be described as the process by which an individual in the financial markets either holds the short or long position for a period exceeding a single trading session. However, the position held by a swing trader does not always go past more than a couple of months. The aim of a swing trade is always to capture profits in the financial markets on a long term basis. Therefore, there are several trades that can go up to a couple of months and still be considered as swing trades.

The large price moves experience in the financial markets is the major target of swing trading. There are several financial instruments that swing trade has invested in. There are two kinds of swing traders those investors who chose to invest in volatile stocks while there are those who chose to invest in stocks that are sedated. Volatile forms stocks tend to experience several movements in the market which make them highly profitable yet riskier. It is the exact opposite of sedate stocks which have less movement in the market and are less risky. However, they have a small profit margin in them.

A swing trader is supposed to be able to identify the price movement of assets. He or she can then be in a position to enter into the trade hoping for a major shift to create his or her market gains. This is one of the most popular forms of active trading in the financial markets. An individual uses several forms of technical analysis to help him or her to be able to base his or her market predictions. There are several advantages that the technical analysis gives a swing trader.

The swing trade is done in assessment with the risk-reward basis. The awing trader is always keen when it comes to analyzing the charts of a particular asset he or she is interested in. It forms the basis of him or her to enter into a stop-loss position because he or she can be able to know if he or she will gain from the trade. The risk to reward ratio is favorable if it is one to two or more. An individual experiences losses in moments swing trading when the ratio of risk to reward is two or more to one.

There is a primary reason why swing trading uses a technical form of analysis. This major reason is because of the short term nature of the trades. The occurrence does not hinder the usage of fundamental analysis in this form of trade. The trade requires utmost fines from an individual participating in swing trading. This entails an individual using both technical and fundamental analysis to achieve maximum gains from the instruments one has invested in them. There is a good depiction in the market where a swing trader uses fundamental analysis techniques. One of these situations occurs when an individual spots a stock that has a bullish setup, he or she would want to make sure that the fundamentals of the assets purchased are favorable.

Swing trading tasks an individual to look at the financial market chats after everyone hour to fifteen minutes time variance. This is critical because it helps a swing trade to know when the entries and stop-loss points are in the market. The act of swing trading is very advantageous because one requires less time compared to day trading. This type of trading is also advantageous because it maximizes profits by capturing the bulk in the market swings experienced in the trade. There are people who are only good at using a technical form of market analysis; the process of swing trading can still be successful even if individual sticks to using this as his base to gain profits.

Swing Trading and Day Trading

The trading strategy used by an individual has an impact on which strategy an individual uses in the financial markets. Day trading involves an individual opening and closing several positions within a single trading day while swing trading involves an individual doing several forms of trade in the last days or weeks of the trade. The two forms of trade have the potential of suiting any kind of trader depending on the time he or she has, the amount of capital an individual is willing to trade and his or her psychology.

These styles of trading are both good. The preference is always based on the interest of the trader. The best style of trade is that which goes with an individual's goals and desires. However, there are various differences that are involved between day trading and swing trading. They include:

1. Trading Time Differs

The time frame that is used in day trading has a clear difference to that of swing trading. There is a primary time frame that is used to categorize a trader who does swing trading from a day trader. This is despite both forms of trading requiring an individual using his or her time. An individual carrying out day trading is known for conducting his or her trade for an approximate time of two hours a day. There is also time a day trader will spend in analyzing and reviewing the trend in the market y usage of charts. This can take up to a person an estimated time of two hours. The total time spent in trading and analyzing day adds up to at least four hours a day.

If a day trader wants to trade for more than four hours, he or she might end up doing his or her trade for the whole day.

Swing trading has the potential of using less time compared to day trading. If an individual doing swing trading can be able to get updates and trades of the orders he or she has made. The occurrence comes in to play when a person doing swing trading is selling off the daily charts. This activity cannot be limited or tagged on a nightly basis since it can be conducted at any time of the day. A person is only allowed to conduct day trading in moments the market is active and still open. The trade is restricted to certain hours of the day. An individual is always forced to using swing trading in moments he or she finds that it is difficult for his or her to participate in the selected hours of day trading. It is because a swing trade has the ability to conduct his or her trade at any time of the day.

Swing traders tend to be affected in low levels in events where prices of assets fluctuate. It is because they focus on the bigger picture which is realized in the long term. However, an individual is supposed to be able to study the daily charts and analyze them well. He or she has the potential of placing his or her trades after the markets have closed with ease. Day trading involves an individual place his trades seconds after seconds depending on the market position.

2. Trading Costs

An individual who is participating in either swing trading or day trading cannot avoid trading costs. However, capital requirements differ from the type of markets they are being traded at. A swing trader can start with different amounts of capital depending on the financial instrument he or she is interested in trading. A good example to depict this situation is the financial markets of the United States of America. An account used in trading stocks in this country has to have the least balance of twenty-five thousand American dollars. There isn't legal minimum capital that is placed on a person who is supposed to perform swing trading. However, a swing trader is on the safe zone when he or she has at least ten thousand dollars in his or her account. He or she is advised to have at least twenty thousand dollars in the event he or she is looking to draw revenue from the trade.

There are no legal minimum amounts that subject a person to having when he or she is trading in the foreign exchange markets. However, he or she is advised to having at least five hundred dollars despite one thousand dollars being termed as a perfect start for day trading. An individual who is focused on day trading is advised to start by trading with one thousand five hundred dollars in the foreign exchange markets. Such amount gives an individual potential of entering several trades at once. Day trading futures will be successful if an individual is able to start by using an amount ranging from five thousand dollars to seven thousand dollars. The estimated amount can vary depending on the contracts of the futures. Day trading futures, on the other hand, will take more capital investment than the above quotation. An individual is always advised to have an estimated capital of ten thousand dollars to twenty thousand dollars.

3. Potential Returns

The levels of profits and loss that can be experienced in these two types of trading have the potential of varying. The loss levels that can be experienced in swing trading are estimated to be quite heavy. This is in comparison to the levels of loss that can be experienced in day trading. This means that an individual is supposed to be well versed with the knowledge of positioning and risk management. A person conducting swing trading is supposed to be able to nature his or her trades. It means that he or she is supposed to be able to adjust his or her trade every night.

This is a completely different case to day trading. The profits that are achieved in day trading are gained from the intraday sessions that an individual does his or her trading. An individual doing swing trading has his or her position at zero during most of the time. This phenomenon is experienced during the last moments of trading at a session. The profits or loss is experienced in moments the trade is being conducted. Swing trading is characterized as having huge profit levels and loss levels compared to day trading.

It is because of the nature of trade between the two forms of trading.

4. Market Swings

Swing trading requires an individual to be able to trade overnight. This is a characteristic of high levels of risks. One form of risk portrayed by this phenomenon which is; slow trading hours always has the potential of leading to widening the spread. It can lead to an increase in the level s or risks of an individual's stop or profit levels being infringed at prices that were not planned for. Erratic price action is a common phenomenon in situations that are described as off-hours. It is another form of risk that presents a swing trader. Day traders, on the other hand, tend to be hugely affected by the volatile markets that are present during the trade. These risks are always controlled or averted during the trading hours day trading is conducted.

5. Over Trading Or Trading Volumes

There are risks of overtrading when its levels to day trading. There are times in the financial markets. The occurrence comes in to play when prices of assets tend to move to one side for a very long time. On the other hand, there are risks when it shifts to the side of over-trading. A good depiction occurs when an individual is having a winning streak in the financial markets. It is because he or she is likely to make more trades making him or her emotionally conjoined to the trade. An individual can be able to be biased by neglecting other market signs leading him or her experiencing huge losses. The risks of over trading lessen when it comes down to an individual doing swing trading. It is because an individual position is always open over a couple of numbers of days. The advantage has seen several swing traders have used this advantage to open several positions using varied financial instruments.

How to Start Swing Trading

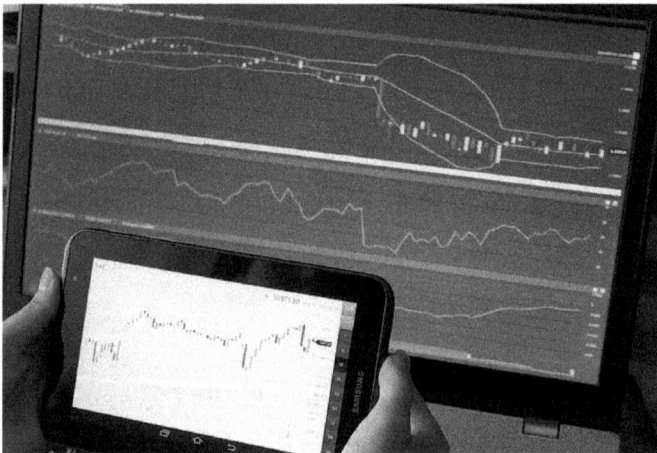

There are several steps that an individual can follow so are to start day trading. However, it is important for an individual to be able to understand the other forms of trading and the financial instruments used in day trading.

Major Forms of Trade

a. Short Term Trading

Time plays a very crucial role when an individual is conducting trade in the financial markets. The expectation of an individual is always anchored by his or her knowledge about time. There are some trading practices that have a better advantage in the immediate future. One of these forms of trade is known as Short term trading which is characterized by trades being conducted in a couple of days or weeks at most. It is favorable to beginners in financial markets since one starts by selling then later buying of assets.

b. Market Order

It is one of the simplest ways for an individual to participate in the financial markets. It involves an individual ordering his or her broker to sell or buy assets at a particular market price. There is no intense analysis in this form of trade since one uses the face value of the financial assets.

c. High-Frequency Trading

Several types of stock trading options are in between inter-trade sessions. High-frequency trading is commonly known to several people in the financial markets. It is also referred to as speed trading. The trick involved in this form of trading is the usage of high-speed computers manipulate the ask and bid prices. Trade is highly automated in this form and is executed in a couple of seconds.

d. Positional Trading

It is similar to swing trading and very popular when it comes to the shorter form of trading in financial trading. It is characterized by ignoring the minor fluctuations that are experienced the price levels of assets.

Financial Instruments

There are several financial instruments that are used in the process of swing trading. They include;

- Options; a contact that gives the buyer the right and not the obligation of buying or selling the underlying asset.
- Stock; it is a financial instrument that portrays an individual's ownership in a certain company.
- Futures; contracts that give a buyer the obligation to either buy or sell an underlying financial asset.
- Bonds; it is a financial instrument that shows an individual loaned amount to a certain institution.

Steps for Swing Trading

The time spent in analyzing the process of swing trading is because it sounds like an overwhelming process. However, there are simple steps that are used in the success of the trade. This is despite the swing trading evolving over the years because of factors such as technological advancements. These steps include;

1. Understanding The Market Environment

Several people tend to focus on the pulse of the market first. It has the potential of putting everything into a good context which forms the base of making good market choices. Several people in swing trading use the Market Health Dashboard to aid in this process. It measures two factors which are momentum and trade on two different time frames. It goes ahead to make is answer across three major averages.

2. Selection of Stock To Trade

Various watch lists are built at this stage based on the stocks that are leading in the financial markets. Firms that are highly performing have their health trends going up and increasing in value. The qualified stocks for trading are got with respect to the market environment. The market scans for stock selection is done every day so that traders do not miss anything in the trading process.

3. Trade Set-Ups and Price Action Analysis

There are three patterns that form the base of swing trading. These patterns include reversals, pullbacks, and breakouts. These are what characterize price movements at any time of the trade-in financial markets. Therefore, the trade is conducted as specific points of these occurrences.

4. Risk Management

An individual in swing trading rarely does huge chunks of trading. It is because his or her investments have the possibility of being exposed to several risks. There are several strategies that help an individual in swing trading to make a sizeable investment portion in order to achieve maximum gains.

Strategies Used In Swing Trading

There are numerous strategies that can be used in swing trading. These strategies are used in the three most important points of swing trading. These points include entry point, stop loss and exit level because they are key elements in this type of trade. The price levels of stop-loss levels and exit points in swing trading are always triggered by the strategy an individual has settled for and he or she is using. Because several technical setups tend to occur depending on the principle that is applied.

The financial instruments that are used in swing trade have time frame couple of days or weeks. This always a good estimated time for the swing to be experienced on the financial instruments. It is great for an individual performing swing trade to be always aware of the time frame he or she has put on her financial instruments. Having this in mind will help him or her to be able to maximize the potential his or her financial instrument in making gains from the market.

There are five strategies that will prove to be critical in the achievement of set targets in swing trading. These strategies are important in helping an individual identifying the opportunities in swing trading. The strategies provide an individual with knowledge of managing his or her trades from the beginning to the end of his or her trade. These strategies include:

1. Fibonacci Retracement

This strategy involves a swing trader using Fibonacci retracement patterns. They have the potential of helping an individual identify support and resistance levels in the market. Such information helps a swing trader to know reversal levels that will be presented on the stock charts. Financial instruments such as stock have the potential of retracing a certain level of percentage within a trend prior to reserving gains.

There are horizontal lines that are plotted using the typical Fibonacci ratios. These ratios include percentages of 61.8%, 38.2%

and 23.6% which depict levels of reversal in a stock chart. There are people who tend to put their focus at the fifty percent level despite it not being able to fit in the Fibonacci pattern. The main reason several swing traders focus on fifty percent is that half of the stock reversal is on reversal.

There are moments were a stock trader can enter into a short term sell position. The reason for this occurrence is because of the retracing of the downtrend in prices of financial instruments. The most appropriate time for this action is when the prices bounce back up to the 61. 8% level of retracement. It is always described as the resistant level. A swing trader is characterized to entering a short position in event pricing levels drops and shift back to the levels of 23.6% which acts as the support line

2. Support And Resistance Triggers

The lines that are presented by support and resistance are the anchorage of technical analysis. A swing trader has the potential of building a successful from of stock trading around him or her. The depiction of support levels shows the price levels on a chart that is below the present market price. At the shown level, prices of stock have the potential of overcoming the selling pressure. This has a resulting effect of a decline in the halted price and the later turning up of price. The best point a swing trader can enter into the trade by buying when their s a bounce of the line. He or she then places his or her stop-loss position under the support line.

The opposite of support is termed as resistance. It is a representation of the prices above the current market prices in the chart. At this point, the market pressure exerted on selling has the potential of overcoming that which is exerted on buying. The prices will turn down from the escalating trend in the event the pressure of selling outweighs that o buying. This phenomenon results in a swing trader into a selling position because of the urge to bouncing off the resistance point. Such occurrence has the potential of placing the resistance level to be below the stop loss point.

There is an important piece of information a swing trader is supposed to keep in mind during the execution of this strategy. The strategy has is very effective in moments when prices have infringed the resistance or the support levels. They are characterized to switching roles in the sense that what was resistance becomes the support and vice versa.

3. Channel Trading

Chanel trading requires an individual to be able to identify a certain type of stock. The stock that is being sported is that which is able to display a strong trend. The stock of interest is also supposed to be able to trend in the desired channel. A swing trader can plot his or her trend on the line of the bearish trend in the financial markets. This will result in him or her to open a selling position in the event that the prices bounce down of the high line of the aimed channel. It is very important to trade using the current trend in moments an individual is using channels while performing swing trading. Several trading positions such as selling positions can be triggered by the downtrend of the financial instruments.

4. 10-And 20- Day SMA

This is another common technique that is used in swing trading. It involves a swing trader being able to use moving averages (SMAs). They are out price data are smooth which are got by calculating and consistently update of the average price. The time frame of the average price can be sourced from a specific rage of time or period. For example, an individual can source it from a span of ten days and divide the value got by ten every day. This is a characterization of the 10 days SMA as it is able to give each day SMA. The values are interconnected as one helps a swing trader to create a smooth line which is responsible to identify specks in the market. The length of time users can be represented in a chart using the same time variance.

SMAs which short lengths are very advantageous to an individual performing swing trading. They help him or her to be able to realize the changes in the prices of financial instruments quite fast and easily. A person can be able to apply either a 10 day or a 20 day SMA in his or her stock chart. One can use the short bars to represent the changes in the 10 days SMA while the long bars can depict shifts in the 20 days SMAs. This helps an individual know when he or she is supposed to sell or buy the stocks.

5. MACD Crossover

It is able to provide an individual with simple ways which a swing trader can be able to swing his or her stocks. It is one of the most common indicators an individual can be able to identify the trend in reversal and direction of stocks. MACD is composed of two forms of moving averages. They include signal line and MACD line; and signals that are generated by the buying and selling when the two lines cross. A bullish trend is depicted when a signal line crosses below the MACD line. The situation makes a swing trader enter into buying of the trade. If a signal line goes above the MACD line, a bearish trend is likely to be portrayed which is a signal for an individual to sell his or her financial instruments.

A swing trader is always patient to wait for the two lines to cross for him or her to be able to have a signal to trade in the opposite direction. This is done before he or she exits the trade. The MACD tends to oscillate between points of zero in the line. Above the zero lines indicates an individual is supposed to buy while bellow the zero line involves an individual selling his or her financial instruments.

CHAPTER 2: ONLINE TOOLS-DAY 3- ANALYSIS

For any trader to be able to succeed in their trading, they have to come up with ways of ensuring that they are not making any kinds of losses. They are required to strategize on ways of studying the market and ensuring that they succeed in their trading journey. There are those tools that they must use in order for them to get positive results even as they study the market. I have discussed some of them below.

Fundamental Analysis

This is a process of looking deeply into the basic parts of the business. This is done because fundamental analysis deals with the most basic part of finances. It analyses the key ratios of the business and finances. It also gives the idea of how the company is dealing with stocks. Fundamental analysis takes in several factors before the analysis. The factors are revenue, assets managements the production of the business without forgetting the interest rates. Fundamental analysis has been used by many investors to check on the health of their investments. They combine it with other tools to determine how worthy the stock they have invested or the value obtained from the stock. The fundamental analysis is all about understanding the key ratios and the terms; this can help you to track all your stocks more intimately and correctly. Fundamental analysis is all about earnings. How much money the company can make in the future and now? The earnings are also referred to as profit. It can be hard to calculate but business is all about increasing earnings which will lead to higher stock price. When there is a fall in the earning, it means there is a problem with the stock.

Total Revenue

This tool is used in business to plan the financial model. It helps you to structure and have better plans for your company. This tool is designed in a simple way to manage the business. It gives one a clear picture of the progress of your business and the growth the business is making and what it will take to sustain that particular business. This tool leads to the establishment of a business plan and strategies.

Once you have a business plan then it becomes easy to track every activity that takes part in the company. You will be having a strong financial future for your company. The revenue tool lays down the current sales made the cost of the sales made and the expenses that you will use for the operations in the company. The importance of this tool is that it shows the income, gross profit and the net profit which can either be short term and long term. You will be in a position to track all the monthly revenue and expenses so that you can find the company running rate.

Price to Earnings Ratio

It is also referred to the P/E, it is used to calculate the value at the market in relative to the stock to the netting while equaling the market rate per share. The profit made in the selling will cater to the supply depending on the profit made. This comparative amount used to calculate what the collection market cost should be and it also predicts the future earnings per share. Those companies that make huge future profits usually expect to get a high bonus or appreciate hoard in the upcoming time. When there is a fair market in the stock this will may the investors to increase the price over time. This helps the investors to know the amount of money they should cater to the supply from what they earned. That the reason the investor would use the ratio and multiply with the ratio because it is called a price multiple. The formula for establishing the price-earnings part is separating the cost charge for each share.

Debt of Equity

The financial liquidity ratio that is used to compare the company total debt to the ratio of sum fairness. The arrears and fair play cost will give the company the proportion in which they get finances from the creditors and the investors. When the company has big arrears to the fairness cost then it shows that the company has many creditors supporting the company than the investor. This is derived by separating total charge by the number of fairness. The cost of equity is considered a balanced cost because it will display all the elements.

Return on the Equity

This is used to measure the company annual return. This is achieved by separating the general income with the cost of its total and it is expressed in proportion. This can also be achieved by dividing the dividend growth rate by what was retained. The return on equity has two parts because it combines the balance sheet and the income statement. There is a relation between equity and income.

Short Interest

It is the number of shares or units that have been sold as a security and they can be repurchased. It is normally expressed in percentage of averaging the daily trading volume. The main reason this is used is that it is in a position to bear what is in the market as a whole and for that specific security. This is one of the ratios that the investors should consider using because for securities with low short interest are less likely to occur the price reject and short compresses. For other analysts, they believe that those securities with higher short interest will likely increase their prices because the short sellers will end up buying a security to cover the short position.

Earnings per Share

It is used to measure the number of money in the net income by each share of the stock. This is achieved by dividing the net income by the number of shares of the stock in the present time. It is used to express the overall profit of the company. The significance of this is that the shares are purchased to earn dividends or to sell them later at a higher price. It is important to the stockholders because of increases in the value of the stock depends greatly on the earnings from the company. It is used mostly by the investors far and wide because they will have to report on the income statement. The only way to interpret the earning per share is the higher the earning per share the show that the investor will reap more when it comes to earnings. That is the reason it should be calculated per year in comparison to the other companies.

Technical Analysis

Technical analysis is a tool that is used when one is examining as well as predicting how the prices are doing in the market. Traders use this tool to when studying the market which enables them to make important decisions about their trading venture. Historical charts, as well as market statistics, are used in the prediction of the market prices. The whole idea of technical analysis is for a trader to be able to learn the market patterns which will give them an idea about how the market is doing. The trader will, therefore, be able to know how the market was doing previously since they will be able to see the pattern clearly through market analysis.

When a trader is planning to invest in a certain market, they are advised to conduct a technical analysis which will enable them to beget a clear pattern about the market price. Once they feel sure about the prices they can decide to trade or wait some more for the prices to become better. They will also be able to predict the price in the days to come through a comparison of the current and past prices. Through the comparison, the traders will be able to know the right time to invest since they know the time when they are likely to make profits and when they are likely to make losses.

There are so many technical analysis tools that technical analysts can use whenever they want to analyze the market. They can use the moving averages, the resistance levels, and the Bollinger bands as well as support. These are the best tools when one is analyzing the market trends and also the market patterns. These are some of the tools that have been tried and proven to give perfect results about the market patterns. They are of great help to them since they are able to understand the charts movements which helps them to easily identify the trends. This makes the work of traders easy since they can see everything clearly on the chart.

There are benefits that come with the use of these tools for the purposes of technical analysis. One of them is that they are able to get signals about the market changes early enough. The signals are of great help since the trader will be able to know when to invest in the market and when to exit it. Most traders have been able to use these tools to analyze the market which helped them to avoid making losses and enabled them to maximize their profits.

The traders are expected to ensure that they have a given methodology which will help them to invest when need be and to avoid investing when the market prices are low. Thorough technical analyses, traders have been able to experience self-fulfillment as traders since they are able to achieve all the goals that they have set within a short period of time. They have also been able to ensure consistency as they trade. This helps them to be able to get the expected profits by avoiding losses.

Technical analysis has become very popular over time. This is because traders have been able to benefit from it greatly. However, the market cannot be always predictable. There will always that one element that the traders will overlook. This element will most likely spoil the pattern which will result in the trader making losses. A trader does not have any guarantee that they will make profits after the analysis because the technical analysis tools cannot be all perfect. They can only predict the market for them.

Traders are therefore asked to use different analysis tools in order for them to be able to get as much assurance as possible. This will help them to manage the risks of loss which will in return enable them to maximize on the profits they make. They need to be armed with other tools in order for them to ensure their security when trading.

Technical analysis has many benefits for a trader. I have discussed some of them below:

- **A Trader gets all the Information**

The price on the market will always give information in regard to a given asset. That price gives a trader a clear picture of what is going on in the market. A trader is able to compare the profits they are making since they can clearly monitor the profits they make through their shares. The trader does not care much about the losses other people make as long as they get more profits each time there are sales. The aim of every trader is to make profits whether the sales are high or low. Everything that is happening in the market is normally reflected on the prices and not on the chart. The trader should, therefore, focus more on the price since it is the key determinant of whether they will make profits or losses.

- **The Prices Move in Patterns**

When prices of shares follow a certain trend, the trader is likely to make money. There will be enough cash flow which will enable the trader to be able to monitor the flow of the cash in the market. By doing this, a trader will be able to make their investment and they will be sure of getting returns in the end. A trader is able to invest once the opportunity arises whether the opportunity is short-term or long term. The investment they make at that particular time will enable them to make some profits which is the aim of every trader.

- **History is Likely to be Repeated**

With technical analysis, traders observe past patterns and compare them with the current ones and use them to make trading decisions. The patterns may not be the same all the time but most of the patterns will be the same over time. The differences are not really that big so a trader may be able to still predict the prices which will enable them to be able to invest wisely.

- **Perfect Timing**

Technical analysis provides a trader with an opportunity for them to be able to time their trades. A trader is able to monitor their trades and invest heavily when the timing is right. A trader will be able to hold their shares without selling them until they are sure that the prices are good enough for them to sell them.

Reading Candle Sticks

Candlesticks are used in analyzing the market too. Traders use them for the purposes of giving a report about the situation in the market. A trader is able to make decisions about their trading venture depending on the pattern portrayed by the candlesticks. They will look at the patterns that occur regularly in order for them to be able to tell whether they should invest in it or not. The pattern gives a little insight about the market trend which enables them to make a decision on whether they should invest in it or not.

The candlestick is said to show how the market is doing just as the bar chart does. It will show the trader the highs and lows as well as the markets opens and the closing price. A candlestick has a real body which is said to be very widespread. It is used for the purposes of giving a price range that is clear. The reading sticks should give the opening price and the closing price of that particular day. One can use different colors to point out the closing as well as the opening prices. When the candlesticks are black, a trader will be able to understand that when they were closing down, the prices were lower as compared to when they opened. When another different color is used, it will indicate that when they were closing, the price was higher than they were opening.

The candlesticks do not have to be black and plain since the traders are allowed to use different colors as long as they help them to differentiate the prices. It is important for a trader to be able to study the patterns as they will help them to be able to enter the market or exit when they are required to. They will also be able to know when they are likely to make profits in order for them to invest at that time. They are also able to tell when they are likely to make losses which will help them to avoid investing at that time.

The candlesticks have become very popular among the traders. This is because the traders are able to easily read them which gives them a clear picture of the market. They are also the most preferred because it is also easy to interpret so the traders are able to interpret them without experiencing any challenges. Traders are able to use the candlesticks before they start trading since they are able to get a clear picture of the market.

The candlesticks are able to show how the current market is and as they form. It does not matter whether the prices are forming at that time or whether the price went up or down within the given timeframe. What counts is the closing and opening price at that particular time. A trader will be able to tell the market price through the candlesticks. A trader observes the movement of the colors on the candlesticks in order for them to be able to tell the price on the market. Where the color positions itself on the candlestick indicates the price of on the market place.

Traders are expected to make sure that they have some knowledge on interpretation of the candlesticks in order for them to be able to understand the changes in the market. They will also be able to tell when the price is high and when it is low. Interpreting the candlesticks well will help them to be able to have a clue on when to invest and when not to. This will help them to avoid making losses and to be able to maximize on the profits they are already making.

There are various advantages of using candlesticks when trading. I have discussed a few below;

Anyone can easily understand them: Candlesticks are easy to understand. Anyone can read and understand them and get the information they may require from them. One is only required to look at the different colors used and make an analysis. Traders with experience and even those without experience are able to go through the candlesticks and analyze the market without experiencing any challenges.

They provide indications of the market turns early enough: A trader is able to study the candlesticks keenly which will enable them to be able to see any shortcomings and rectify them or avoid trading at that time. When the indicators are positive, a trader is able to make a decision on whether to invest at that time or not.

Gives useful insights about the market: Candlesticks are able to show the market changes and reasons for the changes, unlike the other tools. A trader is, therefore, able to make changes on how they trader once they get an insight into the market and reasons why the prices may be going down instead of rising. They will, therefore, be able to change their trading tactics which enable them to make profits in the end.

Reading Bar Charts

Traders are also said to use a bar chart when trading. Bar charts are the easiest tools to use when one is trading since one does not need any kind of interpretation to understand them. Traders use it to show the different prices at different times. The traders use them when they want to learn about market prices at different times. There are bar charts which are used at different times. There are those that are used on a daily basis while there are those that are meant for long term use. A daily bar chart is used when a trader wants to get prices of each day. The bars normally show the opening and closing prices as well as the highest and lowest prices on the market at that particular time.

Through the bar charts, a trader is able to monitor the trends of the prices. This enables a trader to be able to make wise decisions about their investments. They are able to tell the right time to invest since they have a guide about the prices. Traders are also able to spot any potential in trading. This enables them to exploit available opportunities. By doing this, they may find themselves making profits through the opportunities even though they may also make some losses. Prices may go up drastically and the trader to grab the opportunity and invest at that time. They can take advantage of the prices at that time and make as many profits as possible.

Bar charts give a lot of information to the traders. The traders can utilize this information to make decisions about trading. The bar charts are able to clearly show the prices on the market and all the trends. This means that a trader will be able to get a clear picture of where the market stands. It through the trends that the trader will be able to decide whether they need to invest or not.

Through the bar charts, a trader is able to compare previous and current market prices. They will help in ensuring that they get an insight into whether they should invest their money in the current market or not.

Double Bottom and Double Tops

Double bottom and double tops are patterns that are used by traders for the purpose of analyzing the patterns in the market. A double M will be able to tell a trader that there is a reversal on the market trends. A double bottom will help in showing that there is a movement of prices in favor of the trader. This technique is normally used by traders to analyze the market for longer periods of time as compared to other techniques.

Cost and volume

Volume is a word that is used in trading to mean the measure that is given to an asset that has already been traded over a period of time. It is used to tell the number of times that a given item is bought within a given period of time. Volume and cost are, therefore, meant to show the trader the demand for something in the market. it is helpful to them when trading since they are able to evaluate the market through how much they have sold their shares in the market and how many shares out of the ones that are being sold have been bought. This means that the more shares they sell, the more the profits whether the market prices are high or low.

Cost and volume enable the buyer to be able to tell when to sell their shares and when to buy more shares. This is because the more the shares are bought, the more profits they are likely to make. It also means that the lesser the shares that have been sold the more losses they are likely to make. It is important for traders to ensure that they study the market keenly in order for them to be able to trade when the prices are favorable and also when the buyers are many. By doing this, they will be able to make profits when there are many buyers in the market and avoid selling when there are few buyers.

Moving Averages

Moving averages is used in trading for the purpose of smoothening out the price of data through the creation of a constant average price that is constant in all markets. The average price is normally done over a specific period of time. This means that it may take weeks, months or even year for the average price to be given. The trader is, however, free to choose the period of time they would wish for them to get the average price. Through the moving price, a trader is able to focus only on the prices that are moving up. They do not need to concentrate on the prices that are not moving.

It is easy to study the market price through the use of the moving averages because it is clearly shown on the chart. When the prices are way above the ordinary prices, then it can only mean that the market at that time is down. When the prices are under the common moving average, it means that the market trend is down. Traders, therefore, have an easy time analyzing the market through moving averages.

Trading requires a trader to be very keen on the market trends in order for them to succeed in their trading ventures. There is no trader who would want to make losses while trading. They are therefore advised to make sure that they are committed to studying the market with the available tools. A trader is free to choose the analysis tool that they would want to use when analyzing the market.

New traders will need guidance when selecting an analysis tool. This is because they need to learn about the best analysis tools to use in their trading journey. They need to make sure that they are using the most suitable analysis tool when analyzing the market in order for them to succeed in their investment. With proper research about the tools, they will be able to invest when they are sure that they will get returns and avoid those that might make them make losses.

CHAPTER 3: TRANSLATING MOVING AVERAGES-DAY 4- SWING TRADING RULES

Keep it simple

To do swing trading there are basically a lot of strategies one can follow. There so many ways but what are the most simple and effective ways a trader can use in the art of swing trading. From all the strategies that are there then one can use in swing trade then only three are most important in this type of trade. These three strategies help to keep the trade simple even for beginners. This then allows so many people to invest in the stock market through swing trading. So, what are the three most basic and simple strategies of swing trading?

The first point is to take the high position of the market and you go on looking into the market. One will monitor the trends and frequencies of the market. Swing trading remembers, is short term so the period one gets into the market then this is the strategy they use. Go up the market since most people predict that the prices are bound to skyrocket most of the time. There is guaranteed in this type of strategy in which one can get some profit. It also makes one not think a lot about what they are going to do at the end of the day.

The other type of strategy that makes swing trading easy is that one can bet on the low prices. This means that one chooses to get into the market and putting their investment by bidding on the low prices. The chances of prices going high or low are fifty to fifty percent chances. So, meaning bidding on the low prices can also guarantee you a profit. To choose between the two ways one has to look at the former trend and frequencies. These help to guide you on the path you should take on. Both ways are way easy even for a beginner. The final strategy that one can take in swing trading which is simple and effective is the point of having options. This means that the trader should look at all the ways to trade in the swing trading portion and decide on which one he or she wants. Here one has to research all of them but who does not like freedom. Here one will have a lot of points to lean on in the end. If one does not work then they can on something new. This is easy since one does not need to lean onto one thing. This is how swing trading is easy.

With these three strategies help us to figure a way to maneuver the stock exchange market easily through swing trading. There are many more ways to go about swing trade but everyone wants to keep things simple. This is the guide to simplicity in the swing trade. So, for anyone starting in the stock market then take this advice and have an easy way to do things.

Utilize technology wisely

We have become an era that utilizes technology to the fullest. Technology has made our lives very easy in almost all aspects of life. It is no different for the stock market and in this case swing trading. So how does technology help in the field of the stock market? Or how why should we utilize technology wisely? The first reason is that one can get easy access to the market.

There has been an introduction to trading platforms that offer stock market services first hand on your phone or laptop. These platforms are curtsey of the new technology of this era. That means anyone can access the stock market at anytime and anywhere the only things that he or she needs is a smartphone or a laptop. One can trade from any country with a person in another country. See how the internet and technology altogether have made very easy. Another way one can utilize technology is by allowing technology to spark competition. The stock market is already competitive as it is but technology increases that. As competition grows and so does the stock market meaning more money circulating and also more profit to show for it.

Competition comes about in the platforms. That means the platforms keep increasing per day then the platforms will be forced to make their services so that they can counter the competition no matter what. The brokers to face the same challenge and with that, they try to do better for themselves.

The other reason one should utilize technology is that one can have the freedom to trade. Since the platforms are available at the touch of a button then a trader can do all the trading they want at any time they please to do so. Freedom also refers to the point that a trader is free to try his or her own strategies of trading without depending on someone else. Them loses and profits are on their hands. The time each trader enters and leaves the market too is their decision. This is, therefore, the best way to be independent. With technology everything in the world has become fast. In the world of stock market that has happened too. With the platforms in place the selling and buying have been made easier and quite faster. Since people are available at any place and at any time than finding a potential buyer or seller is easy. The trade is also automated any trade is recognized in the shortest time and the confirmation of it happening is available. Most of these trades are seen in e-mail making it very legitimate. One is satisfied with the end result which takes a short time to have.

The final benefit that comes with technology is that it allows people to open up businesses that offer stock market services. These are mainly small businesses that are able to reach the local people. It also helps to show them the ropes of stock market trade.

Use trading capital wisely

The most important thing about investing is the profit one gains and also ensuring that one does not lose the capital he or she has invested. Many people have yet to figure out the right way to invest their capital in the stock market. Some people tend to invest too much without looking at the risk ahead and they finally lose everything they have got. So, going into the stock market as an investment plan then one has to know how to deal with the risks that he or she might face as she gets into the market.

For capital to be used wisely then it has to be invested wisely too. So, what are some of the ways in which one can use his or her trading capital wisely? The important thing to know with capital usage is the fact about knowing where to invest. The first thing anyone should know about the right place to invest in having a keen eye. For a trader, a keen eye is very important if you want to look at any opportunity that is given to you.

A good trader is also supposed to keep their ears peeled to all the business information sources. He or she must know the path that they are to take when it comes to trading. Be there to know about any changes that may affect the stock exchange market. Try to see behind every little thing that may pop up on the stock exchange market. With a keen eye then you can be able to spot a very profitable opportunity. This is the most basic way in which one might end up using his or her capital in good investments.

At the end of it all, he or she gets the profits. The other point is choosing the right company that you can invest in. that means you just do not buy stock for the sake of it. You have to look at how the company is doing. This is where economic-financial issues come in. you have to do extensive research on these uses and then do a clear analysis if the investment is important or not. You have to put in all your options on the table and figure where best can you put your capital. This works closely on with a keen eye since all the information is found in the business segment. When it comes to trading you ensure that you do not use all your capital in one place. That means you should not make one investment and kick back have to take multiple chances since you do not know how things are going to end up in one place. This is done to guarantee that you will not suffer loses. To add up on this one needs to have a backup account. The point is one has to be ready in case things blow up in your face. So, in the stock market have multiple places of investment then you can say you are safe from risk.

Treat swing trading as serious business

If you want profit badly then you need to take trading seriously. This means that when you chose to do swing trading let it not be some game for you. Trading could give you a lot of money if you chose to take things seriously and with the most of keenness.

So, after you make swing trading your primary type of trade then how can you take seriously? This is answered by one understanding of what t swing trade is able to bring to the table. The first thing that will make you take swing trade seriously is the fact that it is accessible to anyone and at any time. This means you can do a full-time trading work with swing trade by your side. It is usually is hectic since it is fast but it is not too fast that new traders cannot keep up. It also allows one to make a few stops to think in the process. This means that every choice you make you have time to think about it and deliberate on it. This basically shows you how good of a way to trade it is. It is a short-term kind of trade meaning that you can easily maneuver your way to getting the profits that you are looking for. If you are serious you will notice an opportunity to get all you want in a moment.

The stock you have while trading you will have to give it up at some point since your period of trade is small. So, one looks at the best deal they can get for their stock. This means one can benefit within a very short period of time. In the market, you will be able to spot the weakness and the strengths immediately if you know all the ropes of a swing trade. Swing trading ropes are easy and even a beginner can learn at a fast pace if they are in deep with the serious trading. Swing trading is for a short time so it should have serious people on its case that meaning there is no time to joke and not do any strategizing. Swing trading requires a plan which a serious person only would have. Finally, one who is taking swing trade should be able to focus on the trade. This because the trade takes just some small amount of time.

With that in mind, one will be needed to focus at that short time so that one can successfully gain some amount of profit. This type of trading is not really for someone who cannot figure how to be serious for even sometimes. So, this is a very serious investment that someone might want to get involved in. this type of trade someone who is swift due to its fast nature but one should also be able to think of the next step since swing trading is basically about swing among your options.

Develop a work plan

For something to work a person should learn the point of making a plan. You cannot just jump into something without knowing how you are going to go about it. A work plan usually helps to make work easier. It also helps one to go for their goals whether daily, monthly or yearly goals. This is something each and every investor should make first before they even get into the stock market. This plan helps you to know what you want and how you will work to get it. Swing trade we already know is short-term therefore this is the first factor that will affect what plan you make. The first thing to making a successful plan then one must understand themselves.

This is where you find your strengths and even weaknesses. This helps tell you what may make your trading advantageous. Find where you can put your own personal charm. It also helps to know what kind of trader you actually want to be at the end. With that information, you will work to achieve to be that trader and all the good qualities that he or she has in your head. For this to work then it must start with you then the plan will be laid out. The other thing to develop your work is understanding that your emotions cannot be part of the trading investment. One must understand that it is important to keep those in check. Emotions are normal and show that one is human but that does not apply in the trading investment. One has to learn how to block these emotions and with that then they can be able to have clear heads to make any choices that concern the stock market. When one is led by sentiment it is hard for them to make choices. They are usually reluctant to let some decisions to make. So, these are the first person things one has to look at as they make a trading plan. The other thing to consider in a trading plan is the goals you as an investor want to reach. The goals are looked into so many things. The factors that affect our goals include: looking at the finances you have at the moment.

The finances show how much you can invest. That means that the less capital you have the less investment you can do. This is important to establish before you go into any investment. You can also figure out how much you want to invest since you cannot invest all of your capital. The other thing to know is how much you want to make once you invest. These profits can be measured with any amount of time that suits you as a trader. This is important since you cannot invest without knowing what you want out of it. The profits should be realistic since you have to measure them up to your initial investment.

Use a stop loss

Every trader is advised to take a stop-loss order once they start trading. Stop-losses a trader when things go downtown south you do not want to end up with losses then this is the right step to take for you as a trader. The stop-loss order means that if the prices of the stock you have in your possession have dropped from the price you bought them at then one's are sold by the broker in charge then a loss is evaded. Once you think the market is safe to go back to then you can be able to return to it. With this order then one does not have to get back to the market to check how his trades are like.

He or she has the assurance of a safe haven if one has trouble what the market trend could bring. This order helps someone who has limited time to keep on checking on all the stocks he or she has. It also works for someone with a lot of investments in the palm of your hands and keeping tabs on all of them is a hand full for them. Stop-loss order also helps people who are in short-term investments since the prices of the stocks can easily go down the drain.

That means one can end up getting loses that are very injurious to one's investment. This is something most people in swing trade try to do which is safe for them to take on. Once you have this then a loss is something you evade and you do not have to worry about that every time you think of your investments. This is an order that most people should think of having once they become traders in the stock market. Stop-loss order is not only used in the case of losses. Apparently, it is also used to predict the prices that are going to come in the future for a particular stock. As it helps in issues of losses it can also spot the profits that one may get in the future. This comes in by reading into the trends, frequencies and even charts of past trades. With this knowledge, one can be a step ahead and know the time they can sell their shares and earn a good amount of profit. This point is beside the normal and usual use of stop-loss we know of so well.

Stop-loss helps to make decisions without having one's emotions coming in. emotions are known to cloud one's judgment. In this case, the option is to sell the stock or go through a big loss and who would want to have a loss. It also helps someone figure the value of the stocks that one has. This is because one has to refer to that value if they are going for profit levels and the loss levels. This order helps someone to be confident and at the top of their game.

Do not risk important things

To understand this better than one has to know what these important things in the stock market are. The important things in the stock market are the profits, the market basically how it is fairing and the stocks. With these three in mind then one knows what they are not mere not missing three are the basic components of the stock market. The buyers, sellers, and brokers are also very important as they are part of the market but the first three make a big constitution of it. So, what are the things that one is not supposed to risk once they join the trading world? The first thing one should not rush into buying or selling any stock. The most important things one is supposed to do is that they have to do a lot of homework before any decisions.

The stock will be there but it is always good to look at all the factors that affect a particular company. If the company is not in a stable place then why risk then earns yourself some hefty losses. This is an important look at the issues that are the particular company try and understand if you are investing there then is the best thing for you. The other thing to consider and not to joke with is your capital. Your capital is the most important thing you have. How you invest it is also important.

People are advised to invest in very different places instead of one place. This is to avoid having issues that one lost all his capital in one investment only. It is easy to depend on a profit from one of the places in which they have invested in. it is also advised that a person should not invest all his money. It is always advisable to keep some for a rainy day.

If it is even possible one should have two separate accounts, one holding money for investment and the other for personal use. This is to avoid someone losing all of his cash by saying he has more to invest in. this is a big concern for those who think that they have a lot to spare. This is an important step. It also shows how much you have invested and in what amount of time. That means you can keep tabs on your capital or your investment.

It is important not to risk anything in the stock market trade. If the stock market is not cutting it for you then you can always leave and find another venture to take on. It is not fair for you to lose all that you have in the name of am trying since one should be persistent in his or her ventures. These impose important things should not be risked should be taken keenly to avoid things going wrong. Stock market trade is very easy to take on and get profit but one has to know the market fully without the exceptions. Do not think it's just charts and graphs since it is more.

CHAPTER 4: HAVE A DEEP KNOWLEDGE OF THE MARKETS-DAY 5- RISK MANAGEMENT

The main reason why most traders do not get maximum profit is that they lack basic knowledge and skills about swing trading. Even those that have it do not use the most up to date strategies while trading. For you to be a successful trader, you need to equip yourself with deep knowledge of the market trends and not just depend on your guts. Most failures in swing trading are not those that have lacked funds or those that use wrong strategies, rather failures are those that did not take their time to understand the market trends. Swing trading is one very risky business if you have not prepared well. One moment you are operating at 100 percent profit and the next you are at the brink of losing all your investments. It all depends on how you play your cards. The kind of company you keep will also determine the scope of the information at your disposal. Always associate yourself with the most experienced players in the field that always have up to date information about market trends and patterns.

Risk Management

Your ability to manage risks ensures that you operate at a profit 90 percent of the time. Risk analysis greatly cuts down on losses. Apart from ensuring a consistent profit, risk management also ensures that you don't run the risk of losing all your money at one point.

The very first step in risk management is getting yourself a reliable broker that is familiar with swing trading patterns. This agent will help you plan your trading keenly before the actual exercise. Remember your level of success will be directly proportional to your level of preparedness. The more time you spend planning the more your chances of making a lot of money.

Know the exact points where you are going to make a profit or loss. Avoid too much gambling and reckless speculation. You can identify these points by keenly analyzing trading charts, make every candlestick count. Ensure that you are in your right state of mind and emotions before you start trading. Maintain that balance of rushing to take up opportunities and being patient to figure out what you are going for. Don't be too excited you make your first profit. Excitement causes laxity and overconfidence and this might affect your future trading activities negatively.

Always ensure that you place one percent or less of your capital in each trade. This ensures that you don't run the risk of losing a lot of money from one trade. Spread your capital among as many trades as you can but at that one percent rate. With a capital of saying a thousand dollars, you can invest ten dollars on each of the trades of your choice. This should not hold you back if you are worth a substantial amount of money. You can as well spend 2 percent of your capital on a stock. Just ensure the amount invested in a single trade is quite small to avoid losing huge amounts of money.

Use a Proven Trading Method

Not every strategy works in swing trading. Only use a method that has been tried and tested. Swing trading is unique and you can't tell what happens next unless you follow a consistent method that has been used before. The following methods have been tried and proven.

Stuck in the box- this is a strategy used when the market has stagnated. This is how it works;

1. Identifies a range market within a particular period.
2. Waits for the price of trade to hit below support.
3. Looks out for the strongest price below the support, this is a rejection price.

4. Once this rejection price is identified, the trader then goes long on the next open candlestick.

5. Make your stop loss below this candle.

Catching the wave- this method involves taking advantage of the most recent pullback when a trend is likely to continue. This is the perfect point to do trading as there is a high probability the trend will continue for some more time before it changes. This is how this strategy works;

1. Identify a trend that matches the 50MA rule.

2. Look out for a bullish rejection as the price approaches the average.

3. Go long on the next candlestick immediately you spot a bullish rejection.

4. Make your stop loss below this candle before there is another swing.

These two methods are the most effective and proven for swing trading. You can also use other methods provided there is a record of their effectiveness. Liaise with the most experienced players in the field to know the kind of methods they use. Avoid those methods that still under experimentation as they can be quite disappointing for a beginner.

Assessing the Risk and the Reward

Risk and reward calculation is the foremost safety technique a good trader must learn. The most successful traders are those that have mastered the art of balancing risks and rewards. They normally do this through agents but there are still those that have perfected it by themselves. Risk/reward calculation is a technique used to kill two birds with one stone. One is taking up prospective opportunities that may appear uncertain and the other is maximizing the profitability of such opportunities in case all goes well. In case the risk backfires, the trader is not supposed to lose a huge amount of money that will bring their trading activities to the knees.

In swing trading, this term means that the trader will be compensated in case they lose their money while investing. The risk-reward calculation is meant to determine whether a particular investment is worth putting your money into. If for example you are meant to invest two hundred dollars in a particular trader, it won't be worth the risk if the compensation is anything equal or less than the 200 dollars.

It makes sense to lose the 200 dollars if you will end up getting more. This the kind of calculation a serious trader should be doing. Stocks with the potential of getting higher prices shortly are more appealing to investors as they see the opportunity to be worth it. If a stock is trading at a higher price than its most recent one, it means that the next time the price drops is the perfect time to buy it. There is a 90 percent chance that the following swing will be towards a higher price. Risk-reward calculations are the only game of probability where you come close to getting your desired results.

The more time and strategies you invest in it the higher the chances of getting what you want.

The best way to carry out a risk-reward calculation is by dividing net profit by the maximum price of risk you are willing to take. Professional investors won't go for a value that is less than 0.15. As an amateur, you shouldn't pick a value that is less than this either. Such kind of stock is not worth the risk.

These are guiding steps for effective risk-reward calculations;

- Carry out intensive research on the kind of stock you want to invest in.
- Use the current price to come up with a lower figure and an upper figure that is going to serve as the yardstick.
- Use these figures to calculate the risk-reward of the trade.
- Try several figures above the lower figure if the ratio is too low until you come with a ratio that is not less than 0.15.
- If you do not come up with a suitable ratio after several attempts, use another stock until you are satisfied.
- Make sure to carry out this kind of calculation every time before you decide to do an investment in a swing trade.

Use a Trading Journal

A trading journal is a device that is used to track all previous trades an investor has done. The secret to keeping a professional journal is by making it as detailed as possible. Include every detail of the trading activities even those that don't seem to be significant. Most traders prefer keeping a normal/physical journal than a digital one. The former is a perfect choice because the trader connects with it. The simple effort of taking a book and pen to put your records down is enough proof that you are into it. However, a digital journal is more convenient and easier to update compared to an actual one.

The purpose of a trading journal is to help you monitor the progress and pattern of your trading journey. It allows you to evaluate strengths and weaknesses in your trading. You can then rectify those weaknesses in future trades and maintain their strengths. Some of the things you must not leave out in a journal are profits and losses. You can also explain why you made such profits and how you plan to maintain that trend. You should also indicate why you made losses and how to correct that in the future. As much as your journal needs to be detailed, also ensure that you only include relevant information to avoid crowding it and make it hard to maintain.

The following is a list of the items that must not be left out in a journal.

1. Date of the trade
2. Name of the stock that has been traded
3. Total amount invested in the stock
4. Description of the trade

5. Various stops used in the trade

6. The outcome of the trade/ whether a loss or gain has been made.

Keeping a trading journal has a lot of benefits to you as a trader. These include:

1. It enables you to carry out a risk-reward calculation for various securities.

2. It helps you to identify your weaknesses and come up with appropriate solutions.

3. It motivates you to look for more information about the market in the form of finding solutions to your shortcomings.

4. A trading journal can be used by new investors as a temporary portfolio where they can evaluate their financial position.

5. A trading journal ensures that you have consistency in terms of your profit margins.

6. It prepares you mentally for all upcoming trading activities as they show you close to what to expect.

7. A trading journal allows you to manage risks more effectively.

8. It enables you to monitor the growth of various stocks in the market.

Keeping a trading journal is specifically recommended for beginners in the stock market. You might encounter some difficulty in maintaining one at first but you will master it within a short time. Experienced traders are also advised to keep a trading journal because it becomes difficult to keep track of all trading data as the activities increase.

Set Stops and Targets

Stops and targets are like traffic lights in the stock market. The former is terminating an interest in a certain stock because its signal is no longer valid. The latter involves setting a respectable profit target wherein you will exit a certain trade upon reaching. These two items also serve as a way of analyzing risks associated with a particular stock. Truth be told, we are all in the market to make gains and if that objective is not being met, you have no option but to exit the market.

Setting stops

You can either exit the market manually or wait until stocks hit your 'stop' value upon which you will have no choice but to walk out with your financial pride still intact. A stop-loss aims to assist you to stay in a trade until the trade setup and original near-term directional bias are eliminated. The objective of every smart trader when placing their stop loss is to place their stop at a level that both give the trade room to move in their favor. Technically, when you are evaluating the best place to put your stop loss you want to think about the closest logical level that the market would have to hit to prove your trade signal wrong.

Therefore, you don't want to put our stop loss unnecessarily far away, but we don't want it too close to our entry point either. We aim to give the market room to breathe but also keep our stop close enough so that we get taken out of the trade as soon as possible if the market doesn't agree with our analysis. There is a thin line that we need to draw when determining stop placement, and indeed we must consider stopping placement as one of the most important aspects of placing a trade. Always give each stop loss placement a lot of time and thought before going ahead with your trading. Most investors disadvantage themselves by placing their stop loss way too close to their point of entry because they want to trade a bigger position size. When you place your stop too close because you want to trade bigger position size, you are jeopardizing your trading edge, because you need to place your stop loss based on your trading signal and the surrounding market conditions, not the amount of money you might be looking to make.

Setting targets

Many traders have fallen victims of their greed by waiting until the market comes crashing on them before they exit. The trick is to exit the market when your ego is still intact. Before you even start trading, come up with clear reasonable targets. Upon meeting those targets, exit the market confidently. Don't be the type to exit out of fear that you might end up losing all your investments if you stayed longer. The emotional part is that its human nature to not want to exit a trade when it's up a nice profit and moving in your favor. It feels like the trade will continue with the same trend so you don't want to exit at that. The funny part is that not exiting when the trade is significantly in your favor typically means you will make an emotional exit as the trade comes crashing back against your position sooner or later. You need to know that you have to make respectable profits of at least 1:2 risk-reward or even more when they are still there. This does not happen unless you have pre-determined before you start trading that you will try to let the trade run further.

Immediately after selecting the most appealing placement for the stop loss, your attention should then be a logical profit target placement and also to risk a reward at the same time. You must be sure there is a decent ratio on a trade. Failure to arrive at this means the risk is not worth taking. It means all you have to do is determine the most reasonable place for your stop loss, and then determine the most logical place for your profit target. If after doing that, there is a manageable risk-reward ratio possible on the trade that particular trade is worth taking. However, you have to be honest with yourself here, don't get into a game of ignoring key market levels or obvious obstacles that are in your way to arrive at a manageable risk-reward from the pressure to enter a particular trade.

The importance of Discipline

In most cases, the difference between the most successful trader and the least successful one is not in the amount of capital each one has but in the level of discipline. This means that you will not be a successful trader without being disciplined in it. It is quite easy to be left behind and miss out on huge profits just because you were unable to manage your funds well. The market is a fast-paced and exciting environment and you can easily get distracted. If you are not careful, the excitement can consume you to the point where you experience extreme emotions. To make the most of your trading, these emotions must be kept at a balance, no too highs and no too lows. This will enable us to remain focused and objective, with the best judgment. Good traders have the discipline to choose between less profitable but reliable deals and those that look lucrative yet shady. Know when to make a move and when to stay back and let the wind pass. Note the following points to help you become a disciplined trader.

Have clear goals and rules from the beginning. Don't just do things because everyone else is doing them. Everyone is using a different strategy that might not work with you as well. Always stick to your script.

Develop an algorithm by which to carry out our trading. This will make sure that you don't do things you have not planned. This will also make sure that you don't get caught up in the heat of the market.

Avoid doing your trading from emotions. Make all decisions with a clear and calm mind.

Keep your plan simple and concise to the point. Complicating it will only confuse when it comes to trading.

Only make alterations to your initial plan when there is proof that such alterations will be advantageous to you as the trader.

Look at the long terms

Most new traders do not know how to tell the difference between various trading periods. You will find an investor treating a short-term as long-term or intermediate and vice versa. A long-term investment option has been associated with long periods that go up to a year while short term investments can be as short as a few hours. The kind of long term we are talking about in this case is in terms of planning. As a trader, it should sink that you are there to make gains for as long as possible and not just a one-off thing. If you treat those trading activities this way, you will be able to make solid plans which include thorough planning and management of risks. The following are the reason you should use a long term approach as a beginner or even an advanced player.

1. It gives you a wider perspective about future market trends. This enables the investor to make long term investment plans and the acquisition of capital.

2. There are few opportunities to focus on as a new trader. This avails you the chance to concentrate resources on one particular objective at a time.

3. Most long term investments require the use of established techniques that are simple to apply. This gives the investor more time plan as compared to short-term and intermediate plans that require new and unique strategies. The new strategies use a lot of time in terms of learning, applying and adapting to them.

4. Long term planning puts less stress on resources and the investor himself. One cannot make good judgment when they are under pressure to trade when they are not well prepared.

CHAPTER 5: BUILDING YOUR TRADING ROUTINE- DAY 6- SWING TRADING STRATEGIES

Swing Trading Strategies

There are specific strategies that you can put in place so that you will identify a trading opportunity. You will be in a position to manage your deals from the word go. You will know the stock you can invest in so that you see the potential in price that will be there in the market. You will know both the present and in the future. There are strategies that you can put in place so that you will have a productive trade.

Fibonacci Retracement

The strategy will help you to know the level of support as well as resistance. You will be in a position to establish whether there will be a possibility of a price reverse pattern.

Support as well as Resistance Triggers

When you know the things that trigger resistance as well as the support in the trading swing, you will be in a position to trade best. You will know how to turn them into strengths, and they will work in your favor. The buying levels higher to the extent of overcoming the selling pressure. At times, the buying pressure is much that it will surpass the selling. When this occurs, the price decline is halted, making the prices to turn back upwards. You need to know the exact time that you have to bring in the support as well as a resistance strategy.

Channel Trading

You need to identify a stock that will display the first movement and dealing within the channel. Make sure that you conduct trade within the trend. When the price takes a downward trend, you need to find for a sell position. Looking for a sell position is significant no unless the price will break out of the pattern. That will mean that it will go to a higher level and showing a reversal when an upward movement begins.

10- and 20-Day SMA

Here is where you make use of the simple moving strategies. The strategy will help you to calculate a constant updating price which will go past a specific period. That will help you to make sure that the price data is smooth as things go on. That will mean that you will add up the closing price of ten days and then divide with ten. You will get the average price out of the ten days. All the averages are connected, and that will create a smooth trend that will make sure that all things go as you have planned. Simple moving averages that have short lengths will have a likelihood of reacting faster to the change in prices than the ones with a more extended period. When the ten closes the twenty, there is a buying signal that will generate as an indication that the prices will go up in a short time. When the ten goes crosses below the twenty, a selling signal will be seen to show that there will be a downward trend in some time to come.

The MACD Crossover

It is a great way to help you to identify the opportunities that are there in the swing trade. It is the most popular strategy that will help you to indicate the direction a particular trend is taking. Whether it is a reversal of an upward movement and has two averages that move from time to time. When the two standards cross, they will lead to the generation of the buying as well as selling signals. The two lines are as well likely to cross above the signal line you have the opportunity to get into the trade. That will enable you to buy any item that you need. Wait for the two paths to cross, and they will create a signal for a business in the opposite direction. You need to be quick before the swing traders withdraw from the trade. These strategies can be put into use and will help you to know the trading opportunities that are there in any market that you have an interest in. Use the best approach to apply these strategies, and you will benefit significantly from them. Seek to find out more about swing trade and the technical indicators and the signals that they show. You will be in a position to predict the price pattern both in the present time as well as in the future.

Trailing Stop and Stop-Loss Combo

There are brokers out there in the market who will do all they can afford so that investors will not suffer much loss. Stop-loss-order is a strategy that is widely known and will always protect you from suffering huge losses. It the price goes down to a certain level, the share will be sold regardless of the current price in the market to make sure that there will be no other losses. For stop-loss to be effective, it needs to be paired with a trailing stop. A trailing stop is a trade order, and it means that the stop-loss price is not fixed to a single dollar amount but is set at a particular percentage or amount that is below the current market price. When the prices shoot, the trailing stop as well goes up. In situations where the price is not rising any longer, the stop-loss will remain in the same place.

That will be a way to shield an investor from suffering losses, and there will be profits realized since the price will get to higher levels.

You can apply trailing-stop in stock, options as well as future exchanges that are there to support the traditional stop-loss orders. You can calculate the maximum risk tolerance when you bring together the conventional stop-losses as well as trailing stops. When the price of a share does up, the trailing-stop will go above the fixed stop-loss, making it be obsolete. When there is a further price increment, it will mean minimizing the potential losses more. There is an added protection, and that will mean that the trailing-stop will take an upward movement. During the regular market hours, trailing will calculate the stop's triggers with consistency.

The trailing stop is hard to apply with active trade because of price fluctuations and the level of the volatility of the particular stock. Fast-moving stock attracts traders because it has the potential to bring forth substantial profit in a short period. For active trade to be useful, a trailing stop value that ca accommodate the usual price fluctuation should be set. Before you get in business, you need to know how the market is for this strategy to work. Being able to time your trade correctly, and it will be of much importance. The trailing-stop is an excellent tool for eliminating and separating you from the emotional part of it that can be in trading. You will be in a position to make the right decisions that you will base on statistical information. There can be lost when you decide to use trailing loss on its own. When you combine with stop-loss, it will be an excellent idea to minimize losses as well as protecting profits.

The idea will help you to reduce losses, get more profit, and the trade will move in your favor. You can choose to use trailing stop in day trading or not to use. The stop-loss order is an approach to use when you want to control the risk levels in a market. If the market is not stable and the prices move in the opposite direction, you can opt to withdraw from the trade. When trailing-stop-loss, you will run the stop-loss up, and the stock price will move upwards. When the price of stock is heading in the right direction, the risk of trade will reduce. When you decide to take a short position in business, and you have a stop-loss, and you decide to trail it, it will be possible. However, you need to wait for the prices to go down.

You need to be careful not to move the stop-loss-order if at all, you are in a short position. That will make you experience massive losses, and you may go to the extent of leaving the trade.

Broker Risk

In some cases, you need something, and you are not sure where to get it. You may be torn in between two things, and you are not sure which is the best. In such a case, you need a broker to help you out. A broker is a middleman who will be in charge of bringing together a buyer and the seller. You will mostly find the brokers in the business world, and they broke aiming to get some commission. A broker can either be a person or a company, and they will arrange transactions on your behalf. They can either be insurance, a commodity as well as stockbrokers.

A broker will be responsible for bringing forth a seller or a buyer and will transact on their behalf. But there are no cases where we can represent them at the same time. They will either provide you with information as well as advice pertaining a particular trade. They will do that at a cost, and that is where they mostly get their income from. That means they have a lot of information and will invest a lot so that they can know more about the trade they are in.

A broker will aim at establishing a relationship with a lot of people that seem to be prospective clients. They will do all in their reach so that they can have the best connections with both the sellers and the buyers in trade and conducts the best deals ever. Research is part of what they do from time to time so that they can have full information at their disposal. Brokers will analyze raw data to establish whether a particular investment is an excellent risk. They will do all they can to provide resources that will help you to manage risk.

They will have full knowledge of what is risk management and how to go about it. They will have numerous solutions for you when it comes to managing risk and ensuring that you minimize the risk associated with a particular trade. They will do all they can to provide you the services that you need. Fixing the risk management tools is what they are best in until it is compatible with the sales process. A broker will not hesitate to teach you or their client how to profit when they apply the risk management tools in the right way. They will do all they can to promote the risk management approaches within the company that they represent in the market. Risk management comes with certain benefits that the brokers are well aware of. You will understand how the whole process will take place with their help. They will know the possible triggers that will interrupt trade, and they will know how to handle each to minimize the possibility of losses.

A broker is a lifesaver. Nevertheless, they can do the things that they are not instructed by the risk management team to do. They will do some things to make sure you are entirely out of the market, and they are there to represent you if you need to go back. Some risks will come along with the broker, and you need to be extra careful when you are dealing with one. Some of the things they will do that pose a risk to your investment are;

Offering the Wrong Advice

They will stand by when they see you making a poor decision, and they know that it is not a good idea. When the broker gives you the wrong information, you are likely to fall, and you will be at risk of withdrawing from the trade. They will stay silent and see you making a mistake if at all, they are not in the best interest of your success.

Not Involving the Risk Manager

Some brokers will have some information that a risk manager needs to know, but they will lock them from knowing it. If they have a good relationship with the executive, they will go through them, eliminating the risk manager from the picture. Lack of knowledge about how important it is to post the risk manager can lead to the downfall of an entire investment if they are not careful. They will assume that they have the best solutions to everything, even on the things that they have less knowledge. When you trust them in such a situation, you will have exposed your trade-in risk. For the chances of risks to be minimal, they need to keep an investor up-to-date with everything that is happening in the market. The things that will possibly interrupt the market in the present and the future should always be their priority. That will help to mitigate risks in case they are a possibility of getting into one.

Regularly Scanning for Trades

As an investor, you need to study how a particular trade is before you venture in since the main aim is to get profit. You can get into a market without its knowledge you end up suffering losses. The need to take time and scan it, then come in. There are numerous software programs that you can have access to, and they can be of help when you need to study for trades. It will be useful if you get the one that has the best features and the one that won't take all the time giving you the results. You will get the data that you require to do the stock technical analysis when you properly scan the trades.

When you scan the trade, you will be in a potion to know which stock is doing best in the market. The product that is moving fast and the specific day it is suitable for you to trade it. You will establish whether there is a gap in the market and the best way to fill it. You will determine whether the stock that you intend to trade has been in the market for quite some time. Scanning for the market regularly will help you know that has an earning and will give you a unique opportunity. The period, the opportunity will last will as well be evident.

Narrow down and make your focus streamline and establish the direction that you prefer your trade to go. You will have more knowledge about how to simplify the process so that you can find good trades and suggested options. You can use technical analysis to find trade if you aim to be in business for an extended period. The signals you will get are likely to help you determine as well as uncover the best trading opportunities. You will know the most consistent as well the profitable signals when you scan the trade regularly.

The approach that you will use to scan the trade is of much importance than how you can choose a stock direction. Be as active as you can and if possible, invest your time and strength so that you will not get into a trade that will later drain you. You would better go a loss while scanning the business rather than getting into business without appropriate information and end up suffering huge losses. You need to know when to be active in trade and when to take things slowly. When the market is not potential, and there is low volatility, that is the time that you need to be less active. When you invest all, you have at such a time, you might end up getting things sour.

When you do a good scan to the trade, you will know when you should not stay at the sideline. When you have no idea the direction the stock you are trading in will take in future, you need to avoid it at all cost. When you overtrade, and the edge is low, you will experience unhealthy portfolio. You need to look for the stock that is having a rise in volatility at the moment. And you consider that as one of the best to trade. A significant positive shift in the underlying stock is all you need to look at when you are scanning the trade. Those are the key things that you need to consider when you go out there in the market to hunt for new trades.

When the volatility level goes down, focus on planning rather than implementing. It is best if you sit on the sidelines when the market is shaking, and you observe as you wait for things to get back healthy. Always be ready to make a move when the need arise so that you can be I a position to compete with others. You will establish who leads in a particular trade and you get to know the direction money is flowing. You don't have to be active only when the market is selling off. When you want to scan for trades, seek to find out about ETFs as well as the overall market. You do not have to forget to observe the charts in trade. If you find that all the conditions are favoring you, plan the trades and do not fear to execute them.

Hot Sector Mania

There are ways in which you can identify the hot sectors in the market, and you use that for your advantage. If you are new in trade, there can be a lot of things that can make you feel overwhelmed. You need to avoid any issue that will make you feel emotional because you have to separate emotions with trade. Emotions will do more harm than good, and the big reason you need to avoid them in every way possible. However, you should not feel discouraged, and you need to know there are ways that you can use to make things quickly as well as useful. Take your time and weigh out on the areas that you want to invest in and the possible return that you will get from them. Do not compare trades and you need to have full information on the trade you are anticipating joining.

If you are a beginner, find out more about the overall trend in the sector that you want to invest your money in. That need to be done before you take a step further to evaluate the specific stock that you want to invest in. You will have an idea of how the trade is doing and the possible strength to put in so that it can be more productive.

The hottest sector is what you need to focus on. Be logic so that when it comes to implementation, you will not have a hard time putting everything on the ground. You can as well focus on a trade that not many people know about it, and you will make much out of it. For you to stay disciplined, you have to put in place a robust trading plan. It will include the types of trade you are considering venturing. It will have the information on when you intend to start the business and the methods you will use to be competitive. You will outline the possible style that you want to apply at the entry-level and hoe you would want to exit the market in the future.

The rules of your trading plan should be laid put in a clear way such that any other person can understand them clearly. Look for the trade that has unique features so that you will attract buyers more easily without having to invest a whole lot of fortune in awareness. Understanding how a particular sector works will be of importance to you, and you will know the approach to use so that you can have access. Get familiar with everything that is run and how it is run. When you get familiar with all that, it can help you to deal with issues in the future in case of any. Stick to the patterns that favor you, and you will reap much out of the trade.

CHAPTER 6: TREND FOLLOWING-DAY 7- GET STARTED

Choosing the Right Market

When it comes to the art of selecting markets, entrepreneurs don't limit themselves. Most of them are confident in their creations aspect and have a prospect of serving a variety of geographies, applications as well as industries of all kinds. Thus, as they make their products, their main target is high and pursue all sorts of strategies to ensure that they feed all sorts of markets that emerge. It is worth noting that the art of choosing the right market is critical in the sense that it allows traders to identify the kind customers they are serving. In other words, once the traders have identified their demands, it becomes simple for them to comprehend the kind of clients they are dealing with. There are different categories of clients in the market. Some are real bargainers, while some will accept the price of the commodities without arguing. Also, different markets are present in the world. However, the traders must select the kind of demands that favors their products.

Pinpointing the Right Market

For trade to be active, the art of demand and supply must be put into consideration. It is worth noting, supply and demand are said to be complete when there are desire and willingness. Thus, a trader will seek to identify a kind of market with high demand. In other words, the traders always try to identify a place with high requirements.

In most cases, places with a high demand for goods and services tend to experience an influx in terms of supply. However, the increased amount tend to be detrimental in the senses that it results in a reduction in the pricing of goods. In such situations, the trader may opt to preserve the products and wait for a better price. It is worth noting that, when traders fail to supply their products, the demand tends to rise with time. An increase in demand in most cases leads to a rise in the pricing of goods. The aspect may cause suppliers to think of increasing their supply. One of the most challenging issues about such elements is that the market is never stable. The other demerit is that traders can`t depend on this market for several reasons. However, seasonal traders tend to divert their products to stay in the market at all times. Although traders aim at identifying relatively stable markets, there are cases where they are forced to accept the demand that is such market and keep supplying their products.

As premises grow and enlarge, firms opt to look for more markets. The approach may involve a simple step such as an advertisement or the art of looking for more customers various on, available online platforms. In such a situation, premises need to employ their services of marketing analysts who spend their time investigating in the best market within the nation. Most of them advise the assumptions about what needs to be done differently. The aspect is critical in the sense that it helps in opening the market as well as increasing the demand for certain types of products despite the increased competition. In other words, market advisors offer the directions that ought to be followed such that organization are able to bring in the same products that are in plenty of supply.

They will sell them in functional processes and maintain their demand via the fact that they are sensitive to branding and packaging. It is worth noting that marketing involves that simple step of welcoming a client. The aspect allows them to relax and will to buy the product at a reasonable price. Thus, other than looking for the best market, it is the role of traders to ensure that the goods they sell are in good quality and packages in a safe manner. The aspect is critical in the sense that it enhances some forms of stability in the market, and better pricing of goods is guaranteed.

Take a look at some of the other aspects that can be used by traders when selecting markets.

Deliver Real Value Quickly

It is worth noting that most customers are sensitive when it comes to the aspect of value. In other words, they prefer markets that provide quality goods and services. Thus, some prefer making their journeys to the market early in the morning before the scorching sunshine destines the quality of some products. The aspect requires traders to avail their products in good time. In other words, timing plays a critical role in identifying the market. A trader ought to gauge the kind of exchange that is available within the vicinity. The other aspect that ought to be considered is the flow of customers. It is worth noting that there are markets that are active in the morning hours while as there are some that are active in the evening hours.

There are also cases where the markets work in shifts; thus, as a trader, it is wise to consider the type of market that suits your product. The aspect is linked to the fact that there are goods that tend to go band of they are left in the sun for a while day. Some require special preservations. There are some profits that excellent they are unpacked firm their initial packages, and they tend to go wrong if nit sold within the right time. Thus, the art of supplying quality goods plays a critical role in enhancing the stability of markets.

Gain access to Multiple Customers

A trader who works within the mercies of one customer risks losing the entire business in case something happens to the customers. In other words, if a trader depends on one customer, there are chances that they may leave the market or goods may be off in terms of quality and the client opt of another trader. However, to avoid such frustrations, the trader ought to diversify the products and work on maintaining some of the loyal clients.

Connect to analogous Industries

It is worth noting that, at times, it becomes challenging to maintain loyal customers. In most cases, when clients get used to a particular premise, there are chances that they may even start taking goods in debt. However, the art of working with analogous clients or industries is critical in the sense that all the parties' trade for their benefit without any intensions of harming the others. Thus, as a trader, it is wise to consider a market that is relatively diverse and one the doesn't foster someone in not trusting a single line of supply.

Choosing the Right Stock

Various factors affect the type of stock that one invests in. Such factors include the level of experience, the capital required, the availability as well as the trading style you want to take. Whether you are choosing a life-time business or rather a time to time commitment over the shares you choose, one ought to be guided by the fact that there are risks that are involved in each case. Thus, as you select the kind of stock to invest in, consider taking some of the risk management processes to minimize the loss in evidence you experience risks. It is good to adopt a dynamic trade. In other words, you shouldn't depend on a single line of products or stock of shares. The aspect is linked to the fact that most of these organizations or instead owners of shares operate under seasonal basis. In that the rate of production of the organization is annual. Thus, the price of the stock from these organizations keeps changing.

One of the best aspects of being dynamic is that seasons differ between different organizations. In that, it is not a guarantee that all organization will have a peak season in the same period. The other aspect that one ought to consider is the strength of the organization. It is worth noting that there are premises which are durable such that even during their off-peak seasons, they do well. Such organizations are worth investing with as their shares to tend to be stable.

Take a look at some of the aspect you ought to consider before picking a specific type of stock;

Consider your Personality

It is worth noting that your personality plays a part in the kind of stock you trade-in. For instance, if you are aged between 25-35 years, your life ought to be active. In other words, the thing you like the things you do and the people you associate with are different from a person who is aged 5o years and above. Thus, you don't expect to stock the same kind of shares. Therefore, before making your own decisions of settling for a specific type of shares, you ought to consider the things you like as well as the activities you love doing.

The aspect is critical in the sense that if you are able to do the things you want, the chances are that you will do them correctly and with the utmost faith. It is worth noting that different stock has different volatility and tend to differ in terms of price. Also, sue to the seasonal in the product of various organizations, the amount of these shares tend to fluctuate from time to time. The aspect is critical in the sense that once you understand that such elements occur in the stock exchange market, you will cope up as you know well you are doing the things in life that you cherish. Thus, follow your personality as you select the stock to invest in.

Risk Management Strategies

It is wise to remember that you are entering into a business zone where risks, lose, and profits are some of the aspects you can't avoid. In other words, in each business, the investments that one makes are more of risks. In other words, you risk your money to either get profit or suffer a loss. Thus, it is wise not to engage in kind of risk you can't manage. In other words, you need to focus on some of the strategies that are aimed at increasing the capital and minimize risks. It is good to invest with organizations that are well known rather than organizations that are unanimous and operate under secrecy. The aspect reduces the chances that are as a result of theft or fraud. It is also wise to consider the kind of stock you are familiar with. The aspect reduces the time required for learning how the capital works. The element also allows one to use skills and the experience gained over time to minimize risks. Increase the art of acre and reduces chances of losing all your investments.

Keep Simple

If you want to excel, don't complicate issues. Whatever you decide, make it long terms and do it periodically. It is worth noting that each stock has its characteristics. Thus, before engaging in any transaction, make a point of learning and understanding all the aspect that pertains a share before starting it over. Also, make a pit of starting to study the behaviors of each stock and advance progressively. Don't start with the art of amassing numerous shares with the aim of making supernormal profits.

Finding a Trusted Broker

A broker refers to a firm or somewhat an individual who charges a certain fee or rather a commission for executing the buying and the selling process. In other words, they play the role of connecting the customer and the seller of the product. Thus, they are generally paid for acting as a link between the two parties. For instance, a client might be willing to buy shares from a particular organization. However, he might be lacking enough information about the places that he can purchase these shares. Thus, he will be forced to seek a person who understands well the stock exchange markets. The broker will, therefore, educate the client as well as link them with the right sellers.

If you want to venture in Forex trading, you will need a person to guide you throughout the process. Working with a broker can be extremely helpful. However, it might be risky considering that there some who advisors who mislead people for their clients for their benefit. The other aspect you ought to consider before choosing a broker is the company you want to work with. The element is due to the fact that the reputation of the organization plays a more prominent role in determining whether the stock will excel or not.

The art of transparency is critical in determining how comfortable one is. In other words, if a broker is known for having a good reputation, the chances are that you will easily trust them. There have been a lot of challenges over the art of trust among many brokers. The volatility, as well as the lack of critical regulations that govern some of these brokers, has been the major challenge. Although there have been bodies trying to regulate the usage of these brokers, the art of technology has affected its effort.

The aspect is linked to the fact that nowadays, a lot of clients are getting their brokers on their online platforms. Some of them can't be trusted while some are real conmen. The aspect has created a lot of problems among traders. Thus, there are a lot of issues that ought to be considered before selecting a broker. Take a look at some of the critical aspects:

Security

The first and most vital aspect that ought to be considered is security. A good broker offers the highest level of protection. In other words, the clients look for a situation where they will feel that they have more confidence, and they can invest their funds without fear.

Transaction Costs

Each transaction requires funds to be effective. In a situation where brokers are involved as intermediaries, the price tends to rise. Thus, it is critical to determine the cash required before giving in to individual brokers. Since there are many brokers, it is wise

Legitimate Brokers

Although numerous brokers have been working in the forex industry, the aspect of legitimacy has been an issue affecting the progress of some these premises. One of the elements that are considered is the vulnerability of the clients.

In most cases premises illegitimate brokers tend to rob of their customers. Most of them are self-reliant and optimistic. Most of them operate above their financial knowledge hence making numerous mistakes. Most of these organization record big loses as they are relatively weak in term of management. The organization offers a lot of transactions that tend to be cumbersome in terms of management. It is worth noting that most of their operations aren't legitimate and never approved by the necessary authorities. Thus, when deciding on the kind of forex premises to seek services from, it is essential to consider some factors. Avoid assumptions that are exaggerative in terms of offering services that are above their knowledge. The aspect is harmful in the sense that they provide services that are not well planned hence recording several loses that befalls many clients in the long run. In other words, the drops recorded in the organization.

Although there are numerous illegitimate brokers in the market, there are legitimate brokers who offer excellent services. Most of them provide a few unique functions. In other words, they don't give a lot of transactions. Thus, they can manage their operations and command profits on their premises. The other aspect worth noting is that most of the services are approved by both the clients as well as the governing bodies in the organization. The other issue worth noting is that most of these premises have employed excellent knowledge in a range the progress of the customers. In other words, all their services are focused on advancing the clients.

In a nutshell, when selecting a Forex broker, it is good to consider several factors. It is critical to find whether the premises are approved by both the governments as well as the clients. It is good to view the number of services as well as the transactions that are offered by the premise. The aspect is due to the fact that most of the wrong assumptions tend to provide numerous services that are poorly managed. The reviews offered by the clients of each of these premises need to be considered as they reflect whether the brokers are legitimate or not. Clients of consistent clients tend to offer reviews that are good as the services they receive manage to be excellent. The financial reports of these organizations tend to be considered. The aspect is linked to the fact that they tend to reflect whether the brokers are making loses or profits. It is critical to find premises that record gains since the benefits tend to be high.

Choosing an Effective Strategy

In each situation, the art of being strategic is essential. In such a case, one is required to make definite and sound decisions that are worth copying. One of the critical aspects worth noting is that making the right decision is the only hope for choosing the strategy in the stock exchange market. For one to be effective in the art of making the right decision, it is good to associate with the right people. Positive individuals tend to make the right decisions. Thus, as you look for a broker or strategy that will work to making a point of associate yourself with people who will instill more positivity. It is worth noting that there are people who are dream killers. The art of associating with such people increases negativity, and one may make wrong decisions.

Learning and being open to ideas is one of the aspects that can help one avoid confusions that are associated with the art of making the wrong decisions. In other words, when you are open to new ideas, you will be in an excellent position to understand the merit as well as demerits that are associated with any purpose. For instance, if you are looking for a stock to invest in, you need to listen to ideas that are sound from people who have excelled in the industry.

Take Profits

It is worth noting that the art of making profits and suffering losses is real. However, all business owners, as well as traders of any kind, work with the aim of making profits. In most cases, trader engages in risk activities by investing funds in various opportunities that crop up in any industry. One of the strategies of making a profit is that of minimizing risks and expenses as one capitalizes on adding capital. In the stock exchange market, profits are generated by buying and reselling shares at a fee.

The best way of taking benefits from any transaction is by choosing the right price of the commodities or stock. The amount of a product refers to the cost or rather the value that is attached to it. Price patterns, on the other hand, refer to the formations that appear on a commodity as well as stock charts which tend to show some certain degree of prediction. One of the essential parts in technical analysis is price patterns. It is worth noting that the easiest way to comprehend about price patterns is by first considering what trade action is. In each day, investors, traders, as well as professionals, let alone institutions are involved in buying and selling of commodities as well the exchange of securities.

The numerous types of market participants who buy and sell their products with unique and different reasons. There are also beliefs as well as traditions that surround the art of trading. The aspects create a particular trend that seems predictable hence the development of a pattern.

CONCLUSION

Thank you so much for reading this book till then end, we hope you learned a lot from it! And if you enjoyed the content then make sure to recommend this book to your friends and family as it means a lot to us.

Thank you for making it through to the end of *Options Trading Crash Course*, let's hope it was informative and able to provide you with all of the tools you need to achieve your goals whatever they may be.

The next step to take is to stop just reading and take the necessary action. Do whatever it is that you need to do so that you can ensure that you have made your investment in a trade that will fulfill your aim; which is to make a profit. If you think that you still need some help to get you started, you will need to have a scanning schedule that you need to follow to the letter. You need to layout strict deadlines for some tasks and also the overall completion of the plans that you for investment. When you fail to set deadlines, you may not implement your program, and it may be of no use to spend time as well as resources when making the plan.

Studies show that complex tasks that are broken into individual pieces, including deadlines, have a much higher chance to be completed. When you refuse to set a real timetable, you will find it hard to complete your tasks and you not succeed. Even if it seems as if it is abnormal, go ahead and set your dates for deadlines and the actual completion day. Compete with the indicators that are there for success as well as failures, and you will find the running smooth. After you have completed with all of your preparations, you will be happy you did. Make sure that you followed all the plan that you have laid out to the letter so that it can work as you desire.

Once you are through with the initial preparation, it is much essential to know that they are just that. They are only a part of the extensive training, and you need to go ahead and implement the plan. The best chances for your overall success will come by taking the time to learn as many essential skills to run your trade as possible. You need to use your qualified plan as a springboard to more significant preparations in the future. You will have some peace knowing that you are prepared for anything that will come up when you are in the trade. You will overcome anything that the future has in store for you. You will not suffer unnecessary losses. Profit is all that you need, and that should be your primary focus.

Here's to your day trading success my friend! Cheers!

CPSIA information can be obtained
at www.ICGtesting.com
Printed in the USA
BVHW041509110321
602278BV00012B/1095

9 781801 656016